by Myka-Lynne Sokoloff

SCHOOL PUBLISHERS

Cover, ©Todd Bigelow/Aurora/Getty Images; p.5, ©Todd Bigelow/Aurora/Getty Images; p.6, ©James Marshall/The Image Works; p.6, ©Bettmann/CORBIS; p.7, ©Glenn LeBlanc/Index Stock Imagery; p.8,©Kevin Fleming/CORBIS; p.9, ©Glenn LeBlanc/Index Stock Imagery; p.9, ©Dave G. Houser/Post-Houserstock/Corbis; p.10, ©Kevin Fleming/CORBIS; p.10, ©Bettmann/CORBIS; p.11, ©Freelance Photography Guild/CORBIS; p.12, ©Rick Friedman/Corbis; p.13, ©Peter Finger/CORBIS; p.14, Library of Congress.

Printed in China

ISBN 10: 0-15-350999-6
ISBN 13: 978-0-15-350999-5

Ordering Options
ISBN 10: 0-15-350602-4 (Grade 5 On-Level Collection)
ISBN 13: 978-0-15-350602-4 (Grade 5 On-Level Collection)
ISBN 10: 0-15-357952-8 (package of 5)
ISBN 13: 978-0-15-357952-3 (package of 5)

4 5 6 7 8 9 10   0940   12 11 10 09

Most likely, you've heard of the Boston Tea Party and Paul Revere's ride. These are just two reasons why many people call the city of Boston, Massachusetts, the birthplace of the American Revolution. Come take a walk on the Freedom Trail. This tour will give you a good sense of the history behind the Revolution. You will discover some of the people, places, and events that helped turn the dream of independence into a reality.

## The Freedom Trail

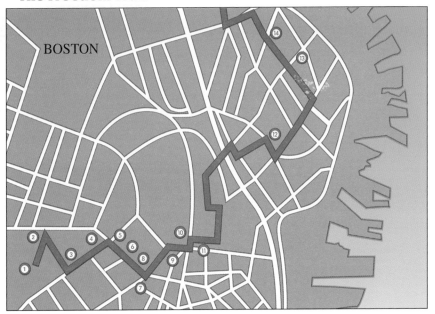

❶ Boston Commons
❷ State House
❸ Park Street Church
❹ Granary Burying Ground
❺ King's Chapel
❻ Benjamin Franklin's Statue
❼ Old Corner Bookstore
❽ Old South Meeting House
❾ Old State House
❿ Boston Massacre
⓫ Faneuil Hall
⓬ Paul Revere House
⓭ Old North Church
⓮ Copp's Hill Burial Ground

## Boston Commons

We'll begin our tour in Boston Commons, the oldest public park in the United States. In 1634, the Commons became a shared space for local people to graze their sheep and cattle.

Here is how the Commons fits into the Revolution: A series of events led the colonists to rebel against Britain. It began when the British government found itself deeply in debt after the French and Indian Wars (1756-1763). Britain turned to the colonies to help get out of the mess the country was in.

First came the Stamp Act in 1765. Britain required many different documents to carry a stamp. Colonists had to pay for these stamps. The colonists appealed to the British government. They felt they should not have to pay this tax, since they had no say in the government.

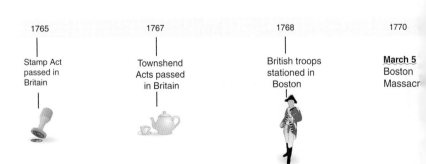

| 1765 | 1767 | 1768 | 1770 |
|---|---|---|---|
| Stamp Act passed in Britain | Townshend Acts passed in Britain | British troops stationed in Boston | **March 5** Boston Massacr |

The Townshend Acts followed in 1767. These acts placed taxes on glass, lead, paint, paper, and tea. Remember that the colonists were British at the time. Drinking tea was a much-loved custom. That tax, in particular, had tea drinkers pretty upset. Protests broke out all over Boston.

As the colonists acted out in anger over the new laws, the British sent troops to Boston to keep the peace. At first, their job was to protect officials from mob attacks. The British troops held drills and marched on the Commons. Later, the soldiers lived in tents set up in Boston Commons. They left from the Commons as they marched to fight the Battle at Lexington and Concord in 1775.

773
|
Act
ssed in
ain
|

|
cember 16
ston Tea
rty

1775
|
**April 18** Revere, Dawes
and Prescott ride to
Lexington and Concord
|

**April 19** Battle at
Lexington and Concord

1776
|
**July 18** Declaration
of Independence first
read in Boston
|

## Granary Burying Ground

All sorts of famous people are buried in the Granary Burying Ground. This place is named for the grain storage building that used to be next door.

James Otis is buried here. In 1761, he argued against laws that allowed the British to search anyone's property for smuggled goods. Here, too, lies Paul Revere, the man made famous by a poem

**Mercy Otis Warren, James Otis's sister, wrote plays in support of the rebellion.**

about his midnight ride to Concord. Those who died in the Boston Massacre are here, too. Also buried here are patriots Samuel Adams and John Hancock, both signers of the Declaration of Independence. In addition, Benjamin Franklin's parents and nine Massachusetts governors are buried in the Granary Burying Ground.

### Old State House

A short walk leads us to the Old State House. It was once the office of the Royal Governor. Try to ignore the skyscrapers that dwarf the building today. At one time, this was the grandest building in Boston. James Otis gave a powerful speech here against the Writs of Assistance, or the rules concerning searches of people's homes. John Adams heard the speech and claimed, "Then and there the child Independence was born."

The lion and the unicorn on the roof were symbols of Great Britain. The Declaration of Independence was first read to the people of Boston from the balcony of this building. It looks over the site of the Boston Massacre.

## The Boston Massacre

Tensions were growing in colonial Boston. Things came to a head in front of the statehouse a few days later, on March 5. An angry mob gathered here and encountered more British soldiers. The mob began to pelt these "redcoats" with snowballs.

It's not clear whether a British officer yelled *Fire!* or *Don't Fire!* to his troops. Apparently, all the soldiers heard was *Fire!* Eleven people were wounded, and five of them died in the scuffle. Among them was Crispus Attucks, an African American who was active in the Sons of Liberty. Today a circle of stones on a traffic island marks the site.

John Adams, Samuel Adams's cousin (and future President of the United States), persuaded others that the soldiers deserved a fair trial. He agreed to defend the soldiers. They received light sentences.

**This stone marks the site of the Boston Massacre.**

## Faneuil Hall

Long ago, Faneuil Hall was the place for town meetings in Boston. Peter Faneuil had built a marketplace for the people of Boston here in the 1740s. Eventually, he added a meeting room upstairs.

The building we see today has been enlarged. Inside is the place where John Hancock and others met to figure out what to do about the hated tea tax.

Soon folks from all over Boston wanted to attend these meetings. Faneuil Hall was too small to contain the crowds. The meetings were moved to the Old South Meeting House, just a short distance away.

Faneuil Hall, home of the idea of no taxation without representation

The statue of Samuel Adams stands just outside Faneuil Hall. Adams was one of the people who planned the revolution.

9

## Old South Meeting House

About 5,000 colonists crowded in and around the Old South Meeting House on December 16, 1773. They were upset about the ships that sat in Boston Harbor, loaded with tea. After long, fruitless talks with the governor, Samuel Adams gave a signal.

Dozens of men disguised as Mohawk Indians were waiting outside the church. They raced to Boston Harbor and climbed aboard several ships that were anchored there. Under the moonlight, they dumped nearly 100,000 pounds (45 kg) of tea into the harbor.

Sometime later, the British took control of the Old South Meeting House. Perhaps they wanted to insult the colonists. Perhaps they just needed riding lessons. The British removed the seats from the church, filled the floor with dirt, and used the building as a riding school!

**Phillis Wheatley, the first published African American poet, was a member of the Old South Meeting House.**

## Paul Revere's House

Walking to the north end of Boston, we come to the home of Paul Revere. This house, built in 1680, is the oldest building in Boston today.

Revere was a skilled silversmith and an engraver. He had a great artistic talent for carving metals. Perhaps his love for metalwork came early in life. At the age of fifteen, he was a bell ringer at the Old North Church.

Paul Revere was also one of the Sons of Liberty. This label identified Revere as a patriot of the colonies. At one point, some feared that the British were heading to Lexington to arrest John Hancock and Samuel Adams. It was crucial to warn them.

After Revere rowed across the Charles River, he and William Dawes made the now infamous ride on horseback to the surrounding towns. They spread the alarm for farmers to prepare to meet the British. The riders were later joined by Dr. Samuel Prescott, and they headed for Concord. Along the way, they were stopped by the British. Prescott and Dawes escaped. Because of their perseverance, the message got through to Concord. Revere, however, was arrested by the British. They later let him go, in time for him to hear the first shot fired in the war.

## Old North Church

A few blocks past Paul Revere's house, and just before his journey, Robert Newman carefully maneuvered up four flights of stairs. Each level leading to the Old North Church steeple was narrower and steeper than the one below. The two lanterns Newman carried made the climb more difficult.

He shone the two lanterns briefly in the steeple window. Then Newman raced down the stairs with lanterns in hand. The young man could hear noises outside the church. British soldiers tried to block his exit. Newman tossed the lanterns aside and escaped by hurling himself out a window in the back of the church. Fortunately, the signal had been seen by those who were meant to see it. Because of it, the riders were able to warn those in Lexington and Concord that the British were coming.

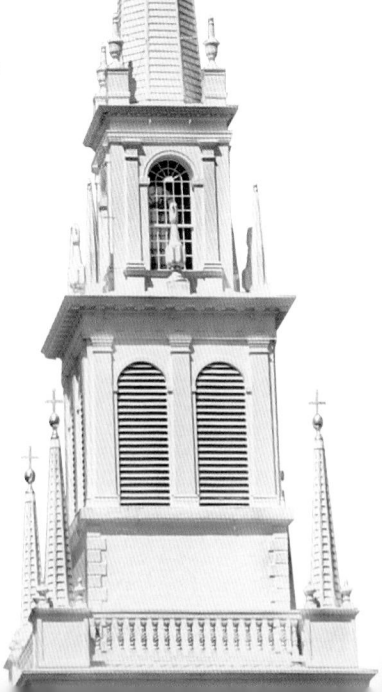

## Copp's Hill Burial Ground and Beyond

As we leave the Old North Church, we'll walk directly up to Copp's Hill Burial Ground. Robert Newman is buried here. From this hilltop, you can also see the Charles River, which Paul Revere crossed in the still, dark night. Across the river is another part of the Freedom Trail.

Our walk along the trail ends here for now. You may want to continue on to visit some other parts of the Freedom Trail on your own. The Bunker Hill Monument is less than a mile across the river. It marks the site of a famous battle of the Revolution.

Before we leave this spot, turn around and look back at the steeple of the Old North Church. Try to imagine just how those two lanterns looked when they shone on that April night of 1775.

**"The Spirit of '76," by Archibald Willard**

"One if by land and two if by sea." The poet Longfellow recalled how Newman signaled the riders about which way the British forces were traveling. "The shot heard round the world" that started the Revolutionary War was fired during the battle the next morning at a bridge in Concord. That shot—and the sacrifices of many patriots—would allow a new nation to fulfill its destiny as a democracy.

# Think Critically

1. In what way is the information in this book organized?

2. What are some of the major events that led up to the American Revolution?

3. What does John Adams' treatment of the British soldiers after the Boston Massacre tell you about his sense of justice?

4. Describe the contributions of three people whose efforts helped the colonies reach the goal of independence.

5. What part of the Freedom Trail tour did you find most interesting? Explain your choice.

 **Social Studies**

**Guidebook Entry** Find out where Bunker Hill is and how it was important in the Revolutionary War. Write an entry about Bunker Hill to add to this book.

**School-Home Connection** Share this book with your family. Talk about places that were important when this country was first founded that you would like to visit someday.

**Word Count:** 1,584 (with graphics 1,715)